MUTANOV GALYMKAIR

The Shining Light

Translated by John Farndon with Olga Nakston

GLAGOSLAV PUBLICATIONS

THE SHINING LIGHT

by Mutanov Galymkair

Translated by John Farndon with Olga Nakston

Publishers Maxim Hodak & Max Mendor

© 2017, Mutanov Galymkair Mutanovich

© 2017, Glagoslav Publications

www.glagoslav.com

ISBN: 978-1-911414-45-2

A catalogue record for this book is available
from the British Library

This book is in copyright. No part of this publication may be reproduced, stored in a retrieval system or transmitted in any form or by any means without the prior permission in writing of the publisher, nor be otherwise circulated in any form of binding or cover other than that in which it is published without a similar condition, including this condition, being imposed on the subsequent purchaser.

MUTANOV GALYMKAIR

The Shining Light

From Rollan Seysenbayev

We are witnessing that there is lot of talented and gifted people in our country. Therefore, our nation, as cultural heritage, is spiritually very rich. The spiritual heritage is closely related to nation`s wealth and prosperity of our Motherland.

We should raise our generation on the basis of this prosperity. This is a key and sacred task of every country. Since only those nations, who have not lost a gene pool of their populations, are the real nations. The rest are just pitying human beings.

Poems of Mr. Galym Mutanov, an eminent scholar, professor, academician and rector of Al-Farabi Kazakh National University, started to be printed in newspapers and magazines. Meantime, the works of Mr. Mutanov have been successfully translated to Russian, Turkish and Arabic languages, published and highly evaluated in these countries.

The favorite poets of the East were at the same time mathematicians, astronomers, geographers and historians.

The famous German poet Goethe himself was fond of the Eastern poets.

Galymkayir poems are inspired by Abay`s works. At the same time Galym`s poems are impressed by

Eastern poetry and characterized by mathematical accuracy. Thanks to that, he can convey several thoughts in two words. Most importantly, his poetry is inspired by high humanity.

The works of Galym were driven by power, property, honor and dignity. Since only a great citizen and poet could inherit and spread honor and dignity into the minds of people.

– Rollan Seysenbayev
The famous kazakh writer, dramatist, translator and founder of House of Abay in London, Abay International Club and Amanat International literary magazine.

Translator's note

The figure of Abai, the visionary, the deeply spiritual poet of the steppe, looms large over Kazakh poetry. Yet polymath Galym Mutanov takes up the challenge Abai throws down – to create verse that is both steeped in the Kazakh tradition of oral verse yet rises to a new intellectual clarity and spirituality. Indeed, Mutanov often echoes Abai's sense of the pain the Kazakh people which deepened immeasurably in the century since Abai's death. "You warrior of verse." Mutanov hails him in his verse 'To the wise Abai,' which laments how Abai was betrayed at the same as celebrating him.

In the range of his poetry, Galym Mutanov truly captures the essence of the Kazakh spirit – from the tough and ageless traditions of the wild steppe to moments of tender intimacy. The measured wisdom and deep sense of morality so intrinsic to Kazakh life of old shines through in verse after verse.

Mutanov wrote all his poems originally in Kazakh, but many Kazakhs speak only Russian. So his poems were translated into Russian by leading poets Vladimir Buryazev and M. Adibaeva. It is these Russian versions that are the source for the translations in this collection.

– John Farndon

The Shining Light

(from the translation by M.Adibaeva)

Fill your life with meaning;
Let the sun come rising!
Amaze with the richness of your soul.
Give your love to people whole.
Love is the highest force, my friend.
Keep it pure in your heart and in the end
Your life's journey will be good –
For its light will shine in the darkest wood.

Allah's gift

We come to this place – Allah's gift,
A sign of his kindness unfurled.
He bestows on us our life's shift,
And brings warmth to all the world.

So then, kindness, not strife,
Is our soul's ongoing call...
And in each small moment of life
To give due honour to all.

Spiritual warmth

(from the translation by V. Beryazev)

A warm heart is a blessing
Of the highest degree.
A man is only living
When his heart is free
To shed its light on another soul.
Nurture another heart,
And back its love will flow
To fill the space forever
With its radiant glow.
For that happy, happy soul
Bathed in warmth and light
Finds the quality of mercy,
And the salt of retribution's bite
Is lost in love's pure victory.
The more hearts that are open
To this gleaming light,
The brighter shines the Temple
Of Creation and the more
Welcome in God's sight.

The Path to Happiness

Allah made all humankind
To be wrapped in a happy embrace.
So in Sharia you will find
Your path through God's own place.

But as men grow, the maniac men
Will pick a fight and slay,
And Truth molesters multiply then
And stray outside faith's way.

To Accept Life

To accept life as it is, as it comes to pass,
Dare to face each detail; count each blade of grass.

Know each nook of Mother Earth,
Her home meadows, woods and skies,
For every rustle of this Great Birth
Is what made you arise.

The Power of Reason

There are limits surely
To thought's capacity.
But the power of reason will
Grind everything in its mill.
Everything in order,
Whether sweet or whether bitter -
It becomes so customary,
It's as if it is statutory.
Of old, life's rhythm shapes
The character a person takes.
If you're not a fool,
Then knowledge becomes your rule.
And its ever solid line
Becomes the base, the spine,
The frame that sees you through
The trials that fate throws at you.
Reason's powerful stream
Will sketch and scheme,
Yet from year to year the tide
Of life flows ever by its side.

Lust for life

The baby in its cradle
Cries with all its might
It's ready for the future
And spoiling for the fight.
The father's always busy,
Pushed this way and that,
Weaving through the smoky press
On the station; he feels flat.
Grandpa's by the cradle,
He looks down and he sighs;
His daring youth won't come again,
No matter how he tries.
Yes, the babe's alive in every pore
As Creation's law decrees.
Burning with a lust for life,
A desire for more and more!

Happiness

In this fleeting life, what does it mean,
To dream of happiness?
What gives you, so proud and keen,
The right to ask for this?
What do we want – no, it's not clear –
Beneath God's sheltering sky?
Yet we boldly ask with little fear,
Rarely asking why.
Yes, happiness has many hues:
But the answer's in a simple call
It is the absence, we should choose,
Of unhappiness – for all!

Born to be happy

Each of us is created,
For happiness it seems.
To reach Him, we're elevated
To strive after our dreams.
We go on always trying.
We have this end in sight,
Like a night moth flying,
Flying to the light.
Yes, our hopes are very high.
We may succeed, or fall.
But there's no other path to try
For mortal man at all.

Bird of inspiration

When the hot furious flame of an idea
Starts to burn deep inside of me,
My soul wakes up. You rise clear,
Unfurl your wings and soon break free!

Bird of inspiration soar in the bright air
And stretch your exhilarating trajectory.
Yes! Relish that long-waited moment there:
Your flight to freedom and victory!

Oh bird of inspiration, be powerful, be strong:
Rise up to the airiest heights of the sky!
Then I might rise with you before too long,
And through the heavens we'll glide – you and I...

Day and night

Day and night, one after the other, on and on.
Allah's will: dark and light, pure and impure, on and on.

Day and night, one after the other, on and on.
God's flowing Creation, its unity, yes or no.

Day and night, speeding after each other, on and on.
Run to the allotted time, yet ride the hour, time after time.

Day and night, changing and unchanging, on and on.
Good follows evil, paradise is golden, remember.

Hope

Thousands of hands lifted each day to the sky
Thousands of eyes raised in hope of reply.
They plead for charity and bread from on high.
They believe He will always supply.

Thousands of palms holding out the great bowl,
Waiting for the cosmos's light.
To feel the Creator, and the unified whole:
The feel of eternity, not a brief flight.

The heart beats, in neither submission nor fear,
And follows the deep rhythm of fate.
And millions, crying out for Allah in prayer,
Pin their hopes that God is great.

A Moment in Eternity

All must perish beneath time's heavy terms,
Yet the river of life, ever flowing,
Renews itself in the light and new germs:
Rise up, shoots! It's time for growing!

The light of love for your father and land
Runs counter to human decay.
It pushes strongly against the living strand
That flows on the other way.

The secret is in lines of descent.
Because each of eternity's instants
Is not a transition from dust to dust, spent,
But a new torch, beaming radiance.

Change is constant. This is clear.
And yes modernity casts a chill.
But be alive while you tenant here;
For when you perish – as you will –
Eternity's variable star shines on.

A Time of Youth

Hope and vigour for a while
Grip the chest... but still the isle,
A happy garden of delight
Filled with flowers and dewy grassed
Where youth skips and waves its hand so light,
Cannot be regained; it's past.

The rolling waves have swept me on...
Far, far away. And now it's gone...
Summers and winters flashing by
Have left a miserable malaise...
And as the autumn bids goodbye
They've quite vanished, those bright spring days.

The seasonal colouring of the Earth
Year after year is given birth
But only once can we poor wights
Tread this living territory.
And when we leave for heaven's delights,
We're nothing but a memory.

New Year

The rain is beating, beating down
                         and streaming everywhere –
Away the last year races!
It's washing all the dross right out and sweeping
                         it who knows where;
Only memory holds the traces.

As usual we will greet the day, and welcome in New Year
To steal our share
Of time allotted us on Earth... And the thread
                         of life will disappear
Beyond the threshold of despair.

What will we take away with us, what will we leave behind,
As we sift away life's sieve?
It's both at the beginning and at the end we find
What life has to give.

We are standing in the rapids. And the blessed
                         miracle of power
Will be swept away, God knows.
Let us be thrown upon the shore of peace
                         when comes our hour –
For life's stream forever flows.

Balance rules the world

The world is held in a balance, it's true;
Both good and evil are even.
Which you choose is down to you -
On the earth or up in heaven.

These scales cannot be corrupted.
They sense each light step of your toe
Every hour of your life will be counted:
Evil and good, friend or foe.
You have free will locked inside you
So always weigh in with the good.
You came into God's home as a man, too.
When you're led out by Allah, you should
Say 'I am a man; it is true!'

Time – the Ark

Time – is the Ark of God. And it's bound,
As every being should know
Straight for the heights of Ararat's mound;
There's nowhere else it can go.

Time – is God's ark on the sea of life
And everyone has their berth.
So be pure for your funeral feast, above strife,
To achieve salvation from Earth.

There's an ark. There's a black and icy abyss…
If sink you plunge lower and lower
So know love. Don't let darkness lead you amiss.
Believe, like the family of Noah.

The sea's whipped to a rage. But the ark of the Lord
Is sturdily built, and it's prow
Is headed securely with all aboard
As the Lord to our fathers avowed.

Common Goal

To everyone living under God's eye
May peace fill your house all the time,
For only Time knows no rest as it speeds on by
For Time alone runs beyond time.

You grow, you grow up and maturity show
Then advanced years as Time streams on,
And in an hour that you'll never know
Comes the time for you to be gone.

We're nomads following the infinite stream,
Encamped on Life and Time's plain.
Everyone knows the end of the dream
But no-one's route there is ever the same.

The Book of Fate

These pages opened with the dawn
And fate will close them up
When the sun goes down.

These pages softly rustling
As each leaf flashes by...
The stream of deeds continues
As the book of life runs on –
We cannot leave a single line
To come back later to.

All that happens to us
Believe me's logged forever,
In this book of life.

Herein lies your testament,
Not to be redeemed nor changed,
And in accordance retribution is
Predestined.

THE SHINING LIGHT

This volume – too long, too short?
Reveals your innermost.
Good alone is our defence
In Heaven.

In the secret hour of Imminence
Whither? Paradise or Gehenna?

We lay the path of our souls
Upon the Scales of Truth.

Human universe

Each one of us contains
The universe entire –
Where all Creation conjoins
And contradictions conspire.
Combining left and right,
Mixing dark and light.
But these ambiguities
Define personalities.
Yet in the absence of clear shapes,
Doubt's dark chasm gapes.
Where is the soul's true place
In this disturbing space?
What in this material night
Can steer us on towards the light?
And yet two beacons ever
Shine over the great abyss:
The heart and mind together
Lead on through the darkness.
So don't abandon hope. No,
Nor relinquish dreaming –
For God to each of us will show
A special vision, A gleaming
Inner world that's only yours.

A Perfect Man

Well, now I'm middle aged and I have stepped at last
Into my second half, it's time...time for a reply
I can't regain my youth and I can't deny the past,
And now my soul is trembling over the years gone by
Like a miser fumbling with the coins he grips fast.
But all that's gone is gone, is gone beyond redemption.
What have I still to do? What more before the last?
Do it, do it now – the good won't be forgotten.
May it be your life, not another's,
                                        that keeps its purpose high!
Never bring yourself down. Always guard yourself firmly.
And keep the injunction, yes, the injunction of Abai:
"A man must strive to be perfect." Strive continually!

A Good Man

It was long the custom for the dead
For the mullah to ask what the living said.
And always they said what they should.
"Yes, the deceased was surely good."

He's gone, and so no matter how
He was, we must accept this now
As fact...and so we pay respect
And speak kind words he should expect.

Good's enjoined by love alone;
Selfish good is in truth a lie
It's enough a good man can be known
If he wasn't evil, and did not lie.

Shelter for the soul

Where does the soul reside?
The soul that brings together as one
The twelve parts of the human body?
Do you understand this secret?
Do you need to see how it's done,
When you live peacefully,
Not bothering to answer, because the whole is the whole.
As long as a person is alive,
They can only feel the soul loving and breathing.
The body is in pain and they believe
The soul was in pain too! – until it flew away.

Beauty

Eight and ten thousand worlds in this universe span!
Then add in besides those Allah made.
Yes! He created it all as his greatness began:
Before us, an unparalleled Beauty was laid.

You can't gaze too long on her radiant glow.
Your eye is drawn in. You gasp with delight.
But this priceless glimpse is all she will show,
For true Beauty always stays hidden from sight.

Yet no matter how fleeting the vision may be,
She lodges forever in your memory,
And though it is dormant, a deep mystery,
Her Beauty's the measure of nobility.

She is all you need for hearing and sight;
Only through her will you truly live.
She's the path to perfection. The road to insight.
And the triumph of mind. This is what she can give.

By all means relish her Beauty revealed:
Her glittering surface, her brightly hued stole.
But to truly know her Beauty concealed
A seer needs to look through the eye of the soul!

Innocence

Oh, if only I could paint as one
The steppeland violet's delicate gleam,
Snowed Altai glistening in the sun,
The singing of an icy stream,
Swans gliding on a mirrored lake,
The copper hues of early dawn,
The scent fresh morning flowers make,
The pale bright curve of the moon newborn...
But they'd barely match in my delight
An innocent girl robed all in white!

A Maiden's Way

Timid eyes. Feelings burn.
No, you cannot hide.
But beware the way you turn;
May fate kindly guide.
Oh, watch them carefully –
The secrets in his eyes.
Be patient – and with humility
You can overcome all desires.

I know that with Allah's aid,
Your forefathers' custom's understood.
You can keep the narrow path they laid:
The path of maidenhood.

With you

It's frightening to think of: what if I had never met you?
Then I'd have never known of love's sweet honeyed bliss.
My life surely would have vanished like early morning dew.
Without love, the soul is wingless; life falls in the abyss.

Every time we meet, I cherish the miracle of you.
Every time we meet, awe freezes in my chest.
Sadness should never quell the fire that glows within you;
It is the soul's true flame, which God has truly blessed.

Would I have ever known loneliness's true pain,
The agony of parting, if I had not known you?
In the dark, I reach for you, again and yet again,
Pleading for the dawn when our separation's through.

My heartbeat's calibrated to the moments we're together
I know without a doubt, I love you, love you, dearest.
I'll be quiet, I'll be patient and get through
                         the roughest weather,
But the only thing I ask is just to have you nearest!

I am with you

When you're rocking and lost in lonely darkness,
Remember, my angel, this is true.
Don't you worry, don't give into sadness:
Just know, dear, I am with you, I am with you.

The moments of life rush by so swiftly
But this is where I'll be when it's through.
Our two souls will merge so completely.
Oh I know I am with you, I am with you.

When you're in the soft shadow of our home, dear,
We'll meet beneath summer skies of blue
We'll find shelter in the light of our souls, dear:
Yes believe me, I am with you, I am with you.

Comparison

(from the translation by V. Beryazev)

The Moon shines in the sky. But you're here, my light!
Your midnight beauty turns the Moon grey.
Let none be offended now when I say,
There never will be a more precious sight.

All people can see the Moon in the night
Brightening darkness with its pallid glow.
Yet its radiance means nothing to me, you must know:
I need you - my only, my one perfect light!

Sorrow

My thoughts go to you, always to you;
My mind rests with you alone.
With my body and soul subservient too,
I've more peace than I've ever known.

But I am bereft when you're not with me;
Vanity and success have no draw.
I'm lost in a desert without water or tree –
Just loneliness's ravening claw.

A soul cannot shed its wrapping and rise
Like a mist floating into the sky.
My life, without you, is just ashes and flies;
It's merely a meaningless sigh.

But if through this time of sorrow for me
You remember to wait and to long
Then like a swift bird, I'll fly – you will see –
To nestle where I belong!

Do you ever think of me?

Do you ever think of me, dear?
Maybe you're close – or far away –
But I will wait through night and day
For a sweet sign to appear.

Do you remember? Will we meet again?
My heart seeks the prize of love begun,
Like a seedling seeks for the sun,
So its aura might never wane.

It will not lose its cherished space –
That unique space in our dreams.
The world cancels time and all its schemes
For true souls to find their place.

Do you remember? Do you think of me?
You were walking, with shoulders bent –
I know how that sweet encounter went –
And dream matches dream, you see.

A Friend

What should a friend be? A simple ask
But how will you answer? What would you say?
People judge you by the friends that last:
Those who stay loyal through the stormiest day.

A true friend of course will wish for you
What for himself he wished he had -
A shoulder when things lie heavy on you,
A support in good times and in bad.

Neither envy nor rage – just sincerity
Will ever force you apart.
Such a soul and true solidity
Is all you need, yes – a golden heart.

And if the whole world could now make friends.
No matter what situation.
We could live again and make amends
Not just numbers but God's true Creation.

Split

(from the translation by V. Beryazev)

They say you can never part body and soul;
They are two halves of an inseparable whole.
But when you go on to the next world in the end
Where is your soul? Where's your body, my friend?

And the soul as well can at times be split:
A half can be pure, but the other so bitter.
And while the first will never need praise.
The other craves flattery all of its days.

Since life began with the Fall long ago,
Within our bodies, a beast can grow.
Believe me, friend, these are not dreams -
Duplicity lies within man it seems...

Others live...

Let honour and conscience slide away
To the recesses of your soul,
Then you reject life in every way
And rush to death's dark hole.

You'll live for evil's sake alone
And blaspheme every day.
For you true peace cannot be known
And serenity's blown away.

THE SHINING LIGHT

When honour is injured

When honour is injured, the soul rises in rage!
Fire roars in the chest to burn up the foe,
The rebel heart pounds in a righteous rampage
And the angry blood boils and makes the eyes glow
With a blazing light...

Enslavement of the Soul

When the blood's drained to exhaustion
Sadness germinates within the ravaged
Soul...
But in time in seclusion
Fully cleansed by righteous rage
Fully awoken by righteous rage
It will revive in fight and courage,
Regain life...
And become whole:
Reborn in Love and Devotion.

The Shining Light

Shadow across the Sun

(from the translation by M. Adibaeva)

Life must bloom in the rays of the sun;
The sun's warmth blesses everyone.
All creatures and plants on the earth, in the sky,
Feel its generosity pour down from on high.

It is the elixir, the nectar, the medicinal glass.
Yes, the sun gives the world every blade of grass.
It is the source of love, the giver of light,
The root of knowledge, the spirit's delight.

Sometimes clouds block out the sun.
On the ground, we see thick shadows run.
And as we naturally fear the night,
All seems ruined by their shadowy flight.

And these dark clouds may possess you,
Not a ray of sunshine will caress you.
And some years it will not be warm
Enough to save their fruit from harm!

Lessons of nature

The rain comes with a delicate blue –
Let God's generosity pour!
But a barren soul, it is surely true,
Stays ever dry to the core…
A seed that falls in a meadow's earth
Is a miracle soon growing green.
But a man not blessed with good will at birth
Shrivels before he is seen.
The blooms of apple quickly fade
To make the sweetest fruit.
Their generous nature is thus displayed
That we might follow suit.
And God is praised by these gentle showers
As their joyful singing brings forth flowers.

After the thunderstorm

Roaring thunder fades away
And lightning's green soon fizzles –
Sprinkling cheeks in heaven's way,
With liberating drizzles.
The clouds disperse. But in the palm
Is only spilled humidity,
While the soul yearning for calm
Is left still parched and thirsty.
The moistured clouds hang in the sky,
But for all their soothing,
The evil ages still pass by,
And hearts still go on beating.

Leaves

Wind whispers out its news now
In every leaves' soft rustle,
In the sacrament of each bough,
In grass's gospel bustle.
A melancholy lull will cast
Its verdict on the chatter.
But if no breezes ever last,
Who tells the leaves the matter?!

Dawn

Moon's lemon honeycomb…
Off-white fingers of the dawn…
Emerging…
From beyond the horizon.
The sun is ready to rise.
Like a newly born star,
It gives its rays to the world.
Life is pleasurable and sweet
With a crown on your shoulders!
What does the future hold?
The thrill opens our eyelids!
We wait for something new and good
With hidden hope…

Dusk

The dusk is slowly falling.
The night is on its way.
In silence, pain comes creeping
As clouds pass on their way.
In the dark embrace of moonlight,
The river goes on flowing –
Drunk on noonday sunlight,
Neither sobering nor slowing.
The whispy smoke of gloaming
Is like a drifting sadness.
In the woods, silence is ringing
As shadows turn to darkness.

The dog barks.

The dog barks
But the caravan moves on,
Always wandering,
Never stopping.
Never heeding
The dog's barking.

Its course plotted and task allotted,
The caravan moves on.
Furious dog.
Barking dog.
Master! See their need and
Give them drink and feed them.

Steadily and stately,
The caravan moves on.
Its steps persistent,
Its nature constant,
It knows its weight.
It will carry its freight.

Yes, the dog may bark,
Yet the caravan will move on.
It holds its course still
And then at last will
See the bright shine
Of the horizon line.

Yet the dog barks
As the caravan moves on.
Barking hoarsely.
Barking breathlessly.
In a cloud of flies
Dust in its eyes.

And people laugh at the dog: "Windbag!"

A Soul and God's Creature

It's just ate and drank since time of the Ark.
Filling its stomach, chewing cud slowly.
Endless rumination is God's simple work
With four legs beneath in a living so lowly.

It's no need for high aims, or a special prize;
It needs to do nothing but labour to eat.
It has only one purpose; it simply tries
To fill up its stomach in the cold and the heat.

So we should be grateful for Allah's kindness
That in all his gigantic creation
He gave only us a radiant mind, yes,
The heavenly way, the soul's foundation.

For nourishment, a soul must feed
On mind and light. A human you were made
To have Love and to search when you need
For the Creator's will displayed.

But if you only live to chew
Then cud's the sole reward for you...

Work!

Even the first step in life
We accomplish through labour.
We can't get up off all fours
Until we wear out our romper suits.
And bread, which feeds us every day,
Needs labour to reap and collect it -
Every moment of the day you must sow or plough
For future times.

No, you cannot live this life
Without knowing toil.
You lose your worth in an instant
As if punched in the stomach,
If you do not have a clear mind or drive
To work, to know and to be!
You are in captivity.
You - are a slave of misfortune,
For you - depend on others...

Mother and child

With what, with what great gift can she,
A mother, hear her son from far away?
Their hearts beat as one, in harmony,
Growing in unison all the way.

But time passes. The son, he grows.
Yet she stays with him, through and through
In summer warmth and winter snows.
It's a mystery. And a law. And it's true.

And when a mother leaves her son
The bond of love and joy will fall.
You're alone, you don't have anyone;
A son cannot find a closer soul at all.

Granddaughter

Our hopes are with you, dear little child.
You arrived like Allah's mercy
In this world of springs and herbs of the wild –
You were a surprise, you see!
We waited long for you to come.
You are so soft and new.
Grass grew over us oldies' fun:
You're a ray of joy, are you!
You've given us smiles of delight again.
You've transfigured our old ways.
We withered reeds are refreshed again,
Now the water of love fills our days.
May the Almighty look after you, dear,
You've revived us all to pray!
Our ancestors' pledge to love and work here,
To strive and create every day,
I give you – and take care not to spoil –
The memory of each generation!
Be a flowering, and stay ever loyal.
Be the glory of our proud nation!
We wish health and happiness to you every day,
And joyful wings for the flight!
We'll be beside you as you make your way –
We wish you success in the fight!

THE SHINING LIGHT

It's important to keep – now and forever –
The blood ties by which we are bound,
So ill luck and neglect and idleness never
Fall on our own family ground.

Nobility

We're endowed with truth and fidelity
But beasts too can have nobility.
Not all are quite so blessed, it's true.
But for some there is a higher goal:
Strong of spirit, free in soul,
In them marked, through and through.

The steppe's great warrior, the old wolf grey,
Who walked the snow and the Milky Way.
Our ancestor, from chief Kekbori born:
Master of the open spaces,
Free spirit of the wildest places,
Guarding the night until the dawn.

You'll never touch the basest lure.
An iron cage you won't endure.
As you await the full Moon's glare,
Howl with the she-wolf – light upon her -
For the eternal: freedom and honour!
They will save you from despair.

THE SHINING LIGHT

As troubles spill from hardship's fount,
Your word of honour's paramount.
"May my life be a pledge, a guarantee."
We respect the grey wolf's dignity
The covenant of his nobility:
A pillar of existence, given free!

Character in congruence

Time speeds onwards, chimes of heaven run their course
And centuries pass as nations learn their ways.
If you're Kazakh, you're born on the mane of a horse.
If you're Kazakh, your road takes numberless days.

The snuffle of the tulpar and the clop of trotting feet
Are the songs of the Kazakh, and when they reach the ear
The true Kazakh's heart trembles and drums out its beat
In time with horses flying, over grass oceans far and near.

Yes, the horse's wild ways run deep in our nation
We have the horse's mettle and its freedom in our veins
Yes, the world is a great herd, and we are all relations
But the argamak alone for us Kazakhs pulls the reins!

Ah, the horse and rider bond together as one –
Just a word or a whinny and at once they'll be racing
Over vast open spaces, wide lands beneath the sun,
Like an arrow from a bow through the air swiftly slicing.

Yes, the world is a great race, where fate decides who's lost
But if the kazanet is your forebear and your one true friend,
Guard your country's freedom and its bread at all cost
And may happiness surround your life's circle 'til the end...

The Grey Leader

Like a swift arrow, at the head of the vee,
Grey wings leads the way
Looking out for his flock – their guide he'll be:
Through wind and through night and day.

He's the first in the flock, first to call and to fly
He knows the east and the west
But his alertness to signals when danger is nigh
Is what marks him out from the rest.

Whenever he hears a faint threatening sign,
He rolls out a guttural alarm,
To warn of the peril, to safeguard his line:
To make sure they come to no harm.

They stretch out behind him both gander and goose
As they glide through the sky homeward bound -
Unless some thoughtless shots are let loose
That strike him down to the ground.

Oh poet seer, so clearly you see:
Like greywings you show us the way!
Your songs promise us that Our Land will be free
Your words bear our true legacy,
   Guarding us, keeping enemies at bay.

To the wise Abai

(from the translation by V. Beryazev)

"Oh, my Kazakhs, my poor, poor people!" -
From the depths of grief, you cried out in pain.
Your friends betrayed you. Yes, this was evil.
How very deep is the human stain!

You tried to lead your people from darkness.
You never yielded though one against hoards.
You warrior of verse! They were lost in blindness:
Infertile ground for your wonderful words.

They are slaves of worldly riches all –
Material comforts their sole delight!
They have the same moral: to grab a fat haul –
Not forgetting to add blood and spite.

They know it all! And no less than those
Who inveigle themselves in the hearts of the wise...
They are digging away like a pigs' nose.
But they're like of pack of dogs in other's eyes.

The dark crows that jostle about heaven's door,
And block the eagle that tries to take flight –
They strut and they fret and they flap and they caw,
Crowding out one who sees freedom's light.

The Shining Light

But the people took his words to their heart:
His wisdom, his guidance, his great sanity.
His voice reaches out a century apart,
As the young hear his Testament at grandfather's knee.

What burned in your soul, you bravely spoke;
It became the Word — our legends, our lores.
Work for the world and ages. Invoke
God – we may fix our century's cause:
"If the will remains in the hands of the people"

Compared to desire

Compared to desire we place
Little value on a life of grace
Or richness of soul. And even when
We leave we try again
To take with us the vain
Hot, army in our train...
We take it...

Formula for a nation's success

The foundation, the very bedrock of progress
In any nation, is good work.
We are all free to enrich or diminish
This treasury with our own labours -
Whether spiritual or material...

Each chooses what he likes
and by these beacons of the nation,
by these treasures, makes a nation strong -
building the weight and measure of civil identity.

Amid the trials of life in a hard hour
Fate - the qualities of our souls
are revealed.
And if someone excels over someone else,
achieving outstanding success in talents or work,
then rejoice! And crush the envy
as it sprouts...
Acknowledge his talents,
and you will lift the spirit of the nation
on a pedestal of victory.

But if envy gnaws and toys with you
and your secret desires are hostile
to your love and friendship...
if you,
wrapped up in your weakness, help hobble
the valourous Kulager-racer,
in which appears goodness and nobility...
This is a blasphemy on the whole nation,
a wound to its spirit and achievements.

Rivalry and envy harm
mutual co-creation. The cure
for envy and contention lies - everybody should know this -
in unity and joint labour.
And in military work or heavy toil or any
creative endeavour - who will argue this? -
there is a formula for success and a guarantee
of the growth of the nation!

Native land

Everyone has their Eden - their own native place:
A desert, a steppe, forests or streams...
And they will see God's heavenly face
As dear memories of it fill their dreams.

You raised me and fed me from the time I was new.
You were the breast that I lay upon.
I will give all my life in service to you
I'll not rest from this moment on!

As time passes by, this gift gains worth.
When you're old, it becomes too hard to bear
To lose, God forbid, the land of your birth.
Oh Allah, lose me finally there
In my own native land...

Atatürk

(from the translation by V. Beryazev)

Through the smoke and fires of hell,
Bloody battles, terrified!
All is past... Yes you rebelled.
Yet you're a pillar, unshakable, dignified.

Did you move on and keep your peace?
What kind of thoughts danced in your brain?
All the trash and rags and grease?
You fought through wickedness and pain.

Yes, you were delayed reaching your goal:
The glorious summit, the thunderous victory!
But you were the guiding hand, the heart and soul
And by force, you threw down the enemy.

You're now imprinted imagewise,
Calling us to drink from a chalice of gold:
In the world of Turks, in the ears, in the eyes, -
A single root and a single soul!

THE SHINING LIGHT

Didn't wait until morning

> *The news of the independence of Kazakhstan came to Turkey at night. Despite the late hour, the government of Turkey recognized it – the first country to acknowledge the arrival of the Independent Republic of Kazakhstan.*

Long lost in the distant mists of history,
Remember us! But don't dwell on our hurt.
Only in the homeland's heart, Ata-Yurt,
Do we keep our deep melancholy.

No, our kin were never lost to sight,
We guarded the steppe, its farms and its soil,
Where soaked the blood of ancestors, and their toil –
The land of our misery's deep twilight.

Er-Turk - our common father and *batyr*!
Centuries have passed before this could be,
But the time has come for us to see
Brothers unite at last without fear.

Blessed under the shadow of Kok Tengri!
Bloodline of Kazakhs - the hour is nigh.
God now releases you from on high.
Kindred spirits near and far are free!

Freedom, the peak of dreams, takes flight.
We didn't wait for the morning. No, we shout
The good news! It's rising! It's ringing out
Far and wide - at the feet of the Kazakh - White Light!

To Mach

(from the translation by M. Adibaeva)
(In memory of Machtaja Cagdieva)

Both old and young are proud of you,
Honoured to be there for you.
For your courage, and your civic view,
Our heads are all bowed down to you.
You are truly loved, and much respected,
"Mach!" we said with great affection.

Then a chasm opened in our view
In the fortieth, people suddenly knew.
We need more than generosity of soul,
Your clean image should be our goal.
It seems to me there's no-one higher,
And to you we should aspire!

God's Plan

In advance, on schedule, our plan is in gear:
We know just what we have to do.
But it is hard work, and it costs us dear.
It's not always easy to see plans through.

That's God's intention. We can't interfere.
Our programme is set from the time of our birth.
To fight it is pointless. The outline is clear:
We must pray to Allah from earth.

Yes, it is true. God presses us so,
But if you're tough and humble, you'll bear it all.
Accept everything, believe it and know:
This is Allah's charge to keep us in thrall.

No matter what happens, how strong your dismay:
Put your back to the whip, stay under the thumb.
That's God's intention, you miserably say.
That is His plan and can't be overcome.

An Old Man

Well there he goes, propped by his stick:
He's old, weak and ready to bend.
The weight of God's questions are coming on thick
He's already nearing his end.

The wheeze in his chest. The snatch at his heart.
The damage of long years of toil.
The weight of the years hangs on each body part
And makes his old spirit recoil.

He turns his face back. He looks round in vain.
His grey head is starting to tremble.
But in his eyes, awkward with strain,
His soul gapes out through each wrinkle.

Remember, my brother, this image of woe.
In a moment, we'll be there too.
Today, it is him. But we've not far to go.
It could be me, your neighbour...or you.

New possibilities

Time after time, year after year,
Adolescence, maturescence and senescence.
One comes after another, weaving and stitching my life.
Adolescent joyfulness.
Maturing reasonableness.
But the hardships of senescence are the start of eternity.
Old age is a universe of occasions
For intimate conversations
With the most gracious and merciful -
With Allah himself…

Mother-Khanum

(from the translation by V. Beryazev)

Amid the crowd you're lonely
You sit – silently, sorrowfully
The days all pass so meanly
In this steppe-like arid valley.
Grey hair curling thinly
Wrinkles on your brow
Furrows of the tests of time
Relentless fate did plough.
Or are your friends now beckoning
From the world beyond?
Was your son lost in the reckoning
And cut his homeland bond?
Your dreams will not come true, you know;
The world deceives in this…
But if you're loyal to Allah, though,
You'll fly over the abyss.
Do not grieve! Between bitter milestones
Find the strength of family ties,
And where you tread upon the earth
Dwell peace and paradise.

Debts and duties

If you borrow from your friends,
They won't forget what you owe,
But to truly serve your people
Is not a debt but your duty.

At your funeral, the mullah asks
 "Does the deceased have any debts?
If they haven't been discharged yet
The relatives must pay them now".

But unfortunately no-one asks
About duties. Do you remember?
Yes, only we ourselves can pay
Our duties, we ourselves alone…

Destiny

Heaven above and the Earth below.
Between them dwells humanity.
Until it is time for us to go,
We are held in life by gravity.

Time passing measures everything.
It measures all from now to then.
Life's soon over. The bell will ring.
You leave when destiny says 'when'.

The leaden soul yearns for the sky,
But coffin dust cannot be free.
To lose the cage of life and fly,
It must be your destiny.

Letters of fate

The weight of life can bend anyone
Whether happy, proud or weak.
You may win, you may lose, or offend someone:
Still fate will mark your cheek.

What matters if your coffin is gold or wood?
Destinies, together and separately,
Announce themselves for bad or good:
"It's written for you, fatefully."

I am prepared. I know about destiny.
I will endure the bitterest test.
I will chop down the birch as it suits me;
In prayer, I'll find my rest.

Everything will pass: I understand.
I believe in my ancestors – and pray
That fate protects my native land.
I will give my soul for it every day.

Horizons

(from the translation by V. Beryazev)

In this world of light and good
God has shown the way -
Between the sky and earth, he stood
The horizon line. He lay
Forces in an elastic state
In day and night the same –
Oppositions that create
An indestructible frame.
We're drawn towards the distant line -
The light of dreams, battle's heat!
And consequently we incline
To where the earth and heavens meet.

A Man is Created Like This

Yes, this is how Allah created you!
The gift he gave is a thirst for a dream.
It will raise you up your whole life through,
Both by passion and fear, it seems.

Once your dream has found its aim,
You fly towards it tirelessly.
It could just be a shadow, and not the same,
Yet your dream will drive relentlessly.
Like a mirage, it lures you on and on
Ridge after ridge, day after day,
You've nearly reached it, and then it's gone,
And the summit's still far away.

You are both ashes and Creation;
Your dream is the very essence of you.
Dream on then without restriction.
But Allah alone makes a dream come true.

Body and soul

At the moment of birth, by the Creator's will,
The body is sent its soul
And they slowly then merge together until
They are one creation, whole.
We are ignited. Then we compete with time,
Each in his body alone...
Our freedom in eternity is our allotted time
Free to fulfill on our own.
The body is like a ship in distress
Waiting to crash on the shore.
The soul must seek shelter in its duress
In the arms of the Creator once more.

The Sea of Life

Tossed on the waves of existence
A soul can never know peace.
Rocked this way and that by each instance,
Each event, that rolls by without cease.
A mountainous wave crashes onwards,
Hurling us out of the way.
Yet even as we are dragged downwards,
We still love and exist every day.

Wave follows wave without pity
There is never a moment's break.
In the storm's eye alone you see clearly,
And for an instant you are awake.

Here in the tempest blown ocean
We live and we sing and we strive.
In an endless search for salvation,
We swim for the light to survive.

Another great breaker soon appears
And rolls back the abyss of the past
And the ebbtide exposes the years
Showing that nothing will last.

THE SHINING LIGHT

Becalm your zeal, float still once more
And measure out the ocean swell.
One day you'll reach the distant shore.
You will have peace. All will be well.
Your soul will be freed.

The Memorial Dinner

My grandmama often used to say to me.
"We're just visiting each other while we live."
And perhaps that explains our hospitality:
The welcome we Kazakhs like to give.

Even through our darkest times of suffering,
This tradition was carried on from the past.
Your guest must always have the tastiest offering,
Even though it could well be your last.

So what have we learned from one another?
Instead of making slaves or an enemy,
Just remember: "We're just visiting each other"
And hold this always a sacred memory.

You're here, then you're gone, then you're laid to rest
But before you depart this world for good
We will bid you goodbye, as our honoured guest
And join you in the finest farewell food.

A leaf torn off

How softly it goes, so soft no-one can tell,
As if it is gently waving farewell.
It glides on the wind, alone always now:
A green leaf plucked from the poplar tree bough.
In the summer air drifting – where? And why?
Others may rustle as they flutter by.
So strange, so early – limp but not dry –
It must have been tired from the sun and sky.
How many questions, as it comes to its end,
Does the green poplar leaf ask then, my friend?
The world is – well it is – simple and clear.
But what is the answer to the question here?

Cloud-driven by the wind

Like a cloud on a gusty day
Swiftly life is blown away
In brief billows, we follow on:
Smoke, a dream, and then we're gone.

This man lived in perfect peace,
Loved and happy till his decease
But then his heartbeat stopped for him.
In an instant, his light went dim.

He left as Allah willed he must:
His body now just ash and dust.

You only know you're mortal, friend,
When your nearest reach their end.

The Caravan of Eternal Life

The long, dusty caravan of life
Vanishes into the distance. Sooner or later
It takes everything and everyone,
Regardless of the flow of time.

The transience of earthly existence
Is shown to us by this caravan.
If this mortal life has a beginning,
Then surely it must have an end.

Pilgrims of the caravan of life!
You will not find an oasis or shelter
On your hard journey through the desert...
Life on this earth has a measure.

The power of fate defines the term
For everyone with its inexorable hand:
With a fatal stamp, everyone is marked:
Some sooner, some later.

True value

It seems happiness must flow
When you're laughing and you're singing.
But only through the bitterest woe
Can you understand its meaning.

You feel active. You feel fit.
You're brave and all-prevailing
But you learn to value it
Once your health is ailing.

You wish everyone the best
And you're kind to all around you.
But you'll know true friendship's test
When betrayal's dirt has found you.

You are alive. You are young still.
You're not ready to be old.
But in time you will be ill
And infirm and feel the cold.

Yes, the dawn brings the day
With its life-giving kiss.
But your friends pass away
And death will never miss...

Under the Shadow of Life

Under the shadow of God now living
Everything flowing, running and changing.
Everything gathered, all that has been,
All that you see and have not seen,
All that is falling and ascending,
Laughter and smiles, tears and sighing,
Whoops of joy, howls of despair,
The light of victory, dark everywhere.
What happened once, what carried on,
What taken with us, what has now gone.
What has been lost, what has been won,
You'll see it all clearly – all will be done!
At last…
At the end of all…

Time is life

(translation V. Beryazev)

You are carefree, thinking,
That life is a honey bowl.
But each taste will leave you wanting,
And regret within your soul.
Look – as your lifetime goes
Flickering by. The days pass.
No dream to reproach you. But who knows -
Will it all end too fast?
Then reflect in anguish and pain
On those days that were empty.
They'll never come again.
Fate won't treat you gently.
Will you see the evil differences
Between your dreams and nature, then?
Will you learn that your dull preferences
Has robbed you of the whole world, then?..
Like a whirlwind swiftly twisting,
Life and time entwine together,
And until death comes calling
We must continue, brother.

Going

So now my dear enslaved ancestors,
I'm going – back to our original earth,
Back to that old unity in things:
To what is eternal and right from birth.
I'm going – to follow solid goals,
To follow, I hope, the right track.
I mean to understand it all
To better this world, this humble shack.
I'm going – to leave my own trail,
To accomplish things on earth,
To cherish with an open heart
All the goodness and the warmth.
I believe – in the worth of man,
In his honour and nobility.
Even in this age, we held this code
And achieved through our ability.
I know – that life is very short,
And for God but an instant.
I work, though – unsparingly:
Each effort will be counted.

I reject – the pursuit of power,
Of riches, and celebrity
I do not wish – to have regrets
As my life reaches its destiny.
And when death strikes and it's time to go,
May I have done my work completely!
Then kindly, in the name of God,
My descendants may remember me…

Life path

(from the translation by V. Beryazev)

Every step.
Is it how you meant to go,
Foot after foot –
Wandering to and fro:
Track, trail, route?
It's the way of the game: you win or lose
Now and then.
At last, neither first nor second; choose
'Pass,' again.
And so we take the pass of Destiny
Over the edge.
And then beyond – slippery and shaky –
The mountain ledge.
Indifferent to sorrow, the world is cunning…
Pilgrim weep!
Life is simply charcoal burning —
Smoke and sleep.

Footprint in the sand

(from the translation by V Beryazev)

A footprint in the sand:
There is one... then one more...
The prevailing wind is strong;
It's in a silent war
To change the sandy steppe
But a scattering of dust
Can never be heavenly manna.
It sooner or later must
Disperse the footprint in the sand.
The wind, and the breathing.
Were they ever visible?
A breath — and then nothing...
You can wander in the desert
With no trace of life or soul...
Look, a mirage of the sands!
Isn't that your goal?

Feeling

There is no time between the shifting of the ages.
The world is unsteady – on a knife edge.
And there is no rest from the burden,
For the troubled, questing soul.
And maybe she is unsettled but
How much more fluid is nature?
We wander a long and winding path –
Impermanence is the essence of everything.

Answer to a question

"When you come before God, what will you say?"
Asks the inquisitive journalist.
And there only is one thing to say:
The humblest, most sincere and purest.
There is just one Creator, all of us know;
He does as he must in his place above.
He will bid the arrogant souls to go,
And bless only those who truly love.
If that miraculous meeting comes to be,
No-one should disdain the call.
Enter this tribunal gratefully
And take your place in God's great hall.
Take courage in your hands and pray;
The message of Creation will persist.
Yes, with a humble heart to Him, I'll say:
"I give thanks, oh Lord, that you exist."

Regularity

The law is universal. The world is bright but strict
Learn to work for the glory of life.
Are you ready to mount each step?

To grow.
To give birth.
To fade.
To go...

There is a monitor for each step.
Who should step? Who should stop?
Who goes the whole journey? Who just a quarter?
                            Who a third?
But everyone lives, hopes and strives.

We dream and wait for dreams to come,
Alive while our time runs on.

We grow.
We give birth.
We fade.
And – we go...

What is needed?

You visited this world and drunk it dry.
What are you taking into God's garden?
What do you need?
A yard of cloth
For your birth
And your shroud...

What else?
Nothing really.
From arrival to departure was not so long.
You're in a rush. What for? What's in your nature?
You didn't understand
Didn't understand the gift.

It would have been enough to just look
The mortal way is always known.

Contents

FROM ROLLAN SEYSENBAYEV 5
TRANSLATOR'S NOTE 7
  THE SHINING LIGHT 9
  ALLAH'S GIFT 10
  SPIRITUAL WARMTH 11
  THE PATH TO HAPPINESS 12
  TO ACCEPT LIFE 13
  THE POWER OF REASON 14
  LUST FOR LIFE 15
  HAPPINESS 16
  BORN TO BE HAPPY 17
  BIRD OF INSPIRATION 18
  DAY AND NIGHT 19
  HOPE 20
  A MOMENT IN ETERNITY 21
  A TIME OF YOUTH 22
  NEW YEAR 23
  BALANCE RULES THE WORLD 24
  TIME – THE ARK 25
  COMMON GOAL 26
  THE BOOK OF FATE 27
  HUMAN UNIVERSE 29
  A PERFECT MAN 30
  A GOOD MAN 31
  SHELTER FOR THE SOUL 32

BEAUTY	33
INNOCENCE	34
A MAIDEN'S WAY	35
WITH YOU	36
I AM WITH YOU	37
COMPARISON	38
SORROW	39
DO YOU EVER THINK OF ME?	40
A FRIEND	41
SPLIT	42
OTHERS LIVE….	43
WHEN HONOUR IS INJURED	44
ENSLAVEMENT OF THE SOUL	45
SHADOW ACROSS THE SUN	46
LESSONS OF NATURE	47
AFTER THE THUNDERSTORM	48
LEAVES	49
DAWN	50
DUSK	51
THE DOG BARKS	52
A SOUL AND GOD'S CREATURE	54
WORK!	55
MOTHER AND CHILD	56
GRANDDAUGHTER	57
NOBILITY	59
CHARACTER IN CONGRUENCE	61
THE GREY LEADER	62
TO THE WISE ABAI	63
COMPARED TO DESIRE	65
FORMULA FOR A NATION'S SUCCESS	66

NATIVE LAND	68
ATATÜRK	69
DIDN'T WAIT UNTIL MORNING	70
TO MACH	72
GOD'S PLAN	73
AN OLD MAN	74
NEW POSSIBILITIES	75
MOTHER-KHANUM	76
DEBTS AND DUTIES	77
DESTINY	78
LETTERS OF FATE	79
HORIZONS	80
A MAN IS CREATED LIKE THIS	81
BODY AND SOUL	82
THE SEA OF LIFE	83
YOUR SOUL WILL BE FREED	84
THE MEMORIAL DINNER	85
A LEAF TORN OFF	86
CLOUD-DRIVEN BY THE WIND	87
THE CARAVAN OF ETERNAL LIFE	88
TRUE VALUE	89
UNDER THE SHADOW OF LIFE	90
TIME IS LIFE	91
GOING	92
LIFE PATH	94
FOOTPRINT IN THE SAND	95
FEELING	96
ANSWER TO A QUESTION	97
REGULARITY	98
WHAT IS NEEDED?	99

Mutanov Galymkair

THE SHINING LIGHT

Translated by John Farndon with Olga Nakston

Publishers Maxim Hodak & Max Mendor

© 2017, Mutanov Galymkair Mutanovich

© 2017, Glagoslav Publications

ISBN: 978-1-911414-45-2

www.glagoslav.com

www.ingramcontent.com/pod-product-compliance
Lightning Source LLC
Chambersburg PA
CBHW021127080526
44587CB00012B/1162